All Around Me

STORYBOOK SERIES

Teacher's Manual

LeapFrog SchoolHouse™

Educational Advisory Board

ISBN 1-58605-848-7

LeapFrog SchoolHouse
a division of LeapFrog Enterprises, Inc.
Emeryville, CA 94608
(800) 883-7430
www.LeapFrogSchoolHouse.com

Table of Contents

Introduction

All Around Me Storybook Series

Guiding and enhancing students' language development is a major goal in every primary classroom. The *All Around Me Storybook Series*, using the time-tested formula of good stories plus good teaching, makes this goal an easy one for busy educators. It is a series that lets a teacher say yes to every student who says, "Please read me a story!"

What guided the development of the *All Around Me Storybook Series?*

- teachers' requests
- interactions with our audience—young children in preschool through first grade
- the latest research on how young students acquire language and begin to learn to read and write

Teachers' Requests

Educators using the LeapPad® platform and books have told us they want simple stories that fit with the themes they use in teaching. As stated in the joint position statement from the International Reading Association (IRA) and the National Association for the Education of Young Children (NAEYC) on the topic of "Learning to Read and Write" (1998), "Experienced teachers throughout the United States report that the children they teach today are more diverse in their backgrounds, experiences, and abilities than were those they taught in the past." This means teachers are looking for a common ground—the types of universal themes featured in the *All Around Me Storybook Series*. These are stories in which all children can find themselves—stories about friends, family, pets, special times, playing outdoors.

Meeting Young Children's Needs

In developing the *All Around Me Storybook Series*, we have stayed close to our audience—children who are 4, 5, and 6 years old. We know what young children like: stories; reading about other children; and interactive materials that make a story more comprehensible and reading more fun. Young children love to have stories read to them. They enjoy being able to access those stories over and over. Because the unique LeapPad platform allows books to come alive at the touch of a pen to the page, children can independently enjoy the read-aloud experience—an experience that research shows to be the single most important activity for future reading success (Wells, G. 1985. *The meaning makers*. Portsmouth, NH: Heinemann; Teale, W.H. and Sulzby, E. (Eds.) 1988. *Emergent literacy: Writing and reading*. Norwood, NJ: Ablex.). Being read to frequently from as young as six months of age has also been proven essential for optimal brain development (*Rethinking the brain: New insights into early development*. 1996. Report of the Conference on Brain Development, University of Chicago). With the LeapPad platform, the read-aloud experience is available to every child.

Latest Reading Research

The No Child Left Behind Act was signed into law on January 8, 2002. It is the product of years of research to find out which methods and materials are most successful in teaching students to read. The research documents that during the critical years of kindergarten to grade 3, the major building blocks for reading success are the following:

- Phonemic awareness
- Phonics
- Fluency
- Vocabulary
- Text comprehension

As you become familiar with the structure of the *All Around Me Storybook Series*, you will see how we have addressed each of these areas. Clearly, the "teacher by your side" assistance provided by the LeapPad platform enables consistent modeling of pronunciations and fluent reading, access to non-decodable vocabulary words, and hidden comprehension aids such as supportive sound effects and dialogue made available by the audio support.

About the Program

The *All Around Me Storybook Series* offers 18 books for the LeapPad platform. The series focuses on content and story to keep students interested and motivated. For each theme, students read two books, each containing three short stories. The first book of a theme has one line of text per page, predictable and consistent sentence structure, and strong picture-to-text correspondence. The second book has more text, greater variation in sentence structure, and a more sophisticated concept load.

The Storybooks

The student books are designed to achieve the following:

- provide many opportunities for language development
- present simple stories about children in everyday situations
- depict common experiences of children in our culture
- introduce new and familiar vocabulary words in story context
- represent many of the ethnic groups now living in America

Teacher's Manual

The *Teacher's Manual* is designed to do the following:

- build background for and excitement about reading a story
- focus on important elements of a story
- offer a variety of activities appropriate for emergent readers, including blackline masters for retelling and further exploring stories
- provide ideas for response, extension, and cross-curricular activities
- foster pleasure in reading

Meeting Curriculum Goals

The *All Around Me Storybook Series* addresses many of the major curriculum goals for language and early literacy typically found listed on state standards, learning continuums proposed by national organizations, and other outcomes-based documents. Teachers will be glad to know that storybook time with the *All Around Me Series* is time that meets needed educational goals.

Curriculum Goal	How Series Addresses Goal
Listening and Speaking	The audio feature of the LeapPad books demands effective listening from students. *Teacher's Manual* activities focus on speaking and listening interactions as follow-ups to story experiences.
Phonological Awareness	Words are clearly and consistently pronounced on the LeapPad platform. Students are able to isolate and hear individual words in sentences. Every lesson plan in the *Teacher's Manual* features a phonological awareness session.
Graphophonemic Awareness	Students have multiple opportunities to match oral and printed words.
Vocabulary Development	The LeapPad books are filled with vocabulary that will help children understand all types of communications about their world.
Print and Book Awareness	In using the LeapPad platform, students are exposed to the left-to-right and top-to-bottom progression of reading, to concept of word, to word-picture identification, and to the physical features of a book. The storybooks feature words both as labels and as part of text that carries meaning.
Literary Response and Comprehension	Because the *All Around Me* books are a storybook series, students are exposed to strong settings, characters, and plots. *Teacher's Manual* activities help students use comprehension strategies such as predicting, comparing and contrasting, sequencing, drawing conclusions, and recognizing feelings.
Writing	Each lesson in the *Teacher's Manual* features a blackline master activity—a written product that students create in response to the story.

Program Philosophy

America's schools are a great amalgam of cultures, beliefs, and learning styles. Yet a basic fact remains unchanged: *All* learners need and deserve a variety of creative, high-quality, versatile materials for enhancing their development as citizens, as English speakers, and as readers.

The Enduring Power of Story

The *All About Me Storybook Series* is based on the belief that stories have power—power to motivate and engage students, power to transmit culture and knowledge. Amid the diversity of today's school populations, stories about everyday experiences help students find a bridge for sharing their ideas and learning new ones. Language develops rapidly and naturally when a child can draw directly on his or her own experiences to understand and relate to a story.

Just reading or listening to a story isn't enough, however. As stated in the IRA/NAEYC position paper "Learning to Read and Write" and supported by research (Dickinson, D. and Smith, M. 1994. Long-term effects of preschool teachers' book readings. *Reading Research Quarterly* 29:104–122; Snow, C., et al. 1995. SHELL: Oral language and early literacy skills in kindergarten and first-grade children. *Journal of Research in Childhood Education* 10:37–48), "It is the talk that surrounds the storybook reading that gives it power." As teachers work with children using the *All About Me Storybook Series* and activities suggested in this *Teacher's Manual*, students revisit a story several times. They might tell a partner about it, or retell it in their own writing. Often, students act out some aspect of a story. They also relate its concepts to other curriculum areas in extension activities.

Making Connections

Themes have long been popular with teachers, especially in the early grades. A theme provides the umbrella, the starting point, from which all kinds of ideas and cross-content knowledge can develop naturally. As students come together to learn about animals, seasons, or weather, for example, they make connections with skills and processes in science, math, social studies, and language arts.

The "classic" early childhood themes address the basic questions every child will spend a lifetime answering:

- **Who am I?**
- **Where do I fit in?**
- **What is my world like?**
- **Who is in the world with me?**

Universal Themes

In the *All Around Me Storybook Series*, nine themes provide the scaffolding for meeting learning objectives across the entire curriculum.

School Everyone who uses this series is learning about school—what a school looks like, who works there, what happens in the classroom, and why it's a fun place to be.

About Me What makes me unique, and what do I have in common with other students? What can my body do? How do I feel about things? Students find themselves in every story in this theme.

Home Everyone has a family, no matter how small. All families have a place to live, no matter how modest. Students discover how their family is the same as and different from others.

Neighborhood Whether you live in a big city, a small town, or the country, you have a neighborhood. It's the people and places you see every day. It's a young child's first adventure in the big world.

Helping Others Compassion and generosity can come easily to young children, especially when they see and read about adults and children who help others.

Animals Pets big and small, forest animals, exotic zoo animals—they're all here. Simple stories about real animals show students the richness and diversity of life.

Nature What makes each season special and fun? What living things are right outside your door? How do plants and animals grow and change? These stories explore the wonders of nature.

Food Everyone eats! Explore colors, textures, and tastes of foods, and find out how they're prepared. Students enjoy foods and fiestas with two children and their families.

Travel In this fast-moving theme, students travel on land, sea, and in the air, exploring new places and ways to get there. Pack your bag and let's go!

The Storybooks

The *All Around Me Storybook Series* accommodates students at many stages of language development. With two overall levels of difficulty, three stories in each book, and 18 books in the series, students have many opportunities to practice their emerging language and reading skills in real story contexts that are developmentally appropriate for them.

The LeapPad® pages are filled with engaging art that closely resembles the images found in typical trade picture books. As with trade books, the art styles vary from realistic to whimsical. All art styles are realistic enough that students can easily associate pictures and meanings.

LeapPad Book Audio Features

The interaction required of students is similar throughout all the books in the series, freeing them from the need to figure out page navigation so that they can attend to the

Using the Level 1 Books ▲

Eager preschoolers and kindergartners will love the pacing of these stories, with their lively illustrations, simple story lines, and limited text. These books are also useful for older students who are just learning English. The interactive format of the LeapPad platform gives students immediate feedback every time they touch the LeapPad pen to a word or a picture.

If students touch the girl's mouth, they hear singing.

Some pages include environmental print, such as the words on this poster.

Stories focus on word-picture identification of objects, locations, and key vocabulary.

Students can look for the main character on almost every page. If they touch him or any other character, they will hear the character speak.

story line, vocabulary, and concepts. The points of interaction are described in the callouts below. Note that students must always begin by touching the GO circle on each spread. This is how the software recognizes which page the reader is on.

What you cannot see on the LeapPad book pages is the audio behind them. For the *All Around Me Storybook Series* the audio has been carefully crafted to do the following:

- introduce and provide contextual information for each story on its title page in English and Spanish
- provide directions on the first spread of each story in English or Spanish
- read the stories in English fluently with correct pronunciation, inflection, and intonation
- read each word as many times as the student needs to hear it
- interweave stories and other audio to create maximum learning opportunities
- offer additional learning opportunities as students touch the characters who talk and use the vocabulary words in context
- increase learning and fun by providing appropriate sound effects that deepen comprehension, such as doorbells that ring
- provide an interactive picture dictionary to review vocabulary

Using the Level 2 Books

Many students are ready for stories with more challenging content and longer, more complex sentences. They can use the storybooks to increase their speaking and listening vocabulary, while also hearing and practicing the nuances of spoken English.

During the first reading, students can explore the pictures as they listen to the text. (Note that unlike an audiotape, the student, rather than the tape, decides when to turn the page.) When students reread the book, they have many options: They can try reading parts of the story along with the audio. They can read some or all of the text themselves. And of course every student will want to explore the pages with the LeapPad pen!

Picture details and vocabulary words focus on key concepts in multiple curriculum areas.

In Level 2 books, students will hear a complete sentence when they touch a story character.

GO

Ana learns math in the afternoon. Today she is learning about shapes.

14

Sometimes the class works together. Today they work together on science.

15

The main character is always part of the action in the illustrations.

More lines of text and more sentences increase the concept load in Level 2 books.

The Teacher's Manual

All the lesson plans for the 18 books in the *All Around Me Storybook Series* are in a single convenient *Teacher's Manual.* The *Teacher's Manual* also includes 18 blackline masters. These open-ended activities are designed to be done independently by individual students or partners and to provide opportunities for the following:

- following directions
- oral language and vocabulary development
- retelling or extending a story
- exploring story-related curriculum content, such as bike safety or animal habitats

A Story Lesson

The goals of the *Teacher's Manual* are centered around exposing all of the learning embedded in the LeapPad® book pages and increasing teachable moments around that instruction. Every lesson in the *Teacher's Manual* contains the parts shown below.

Blackline Masters

Blackline Masters for each book are on pages 18–35 of the *Teacher's Manual.* Students usually work in pairs so that they are gaining practice in listening and speaking, using vocabulary they are learning.

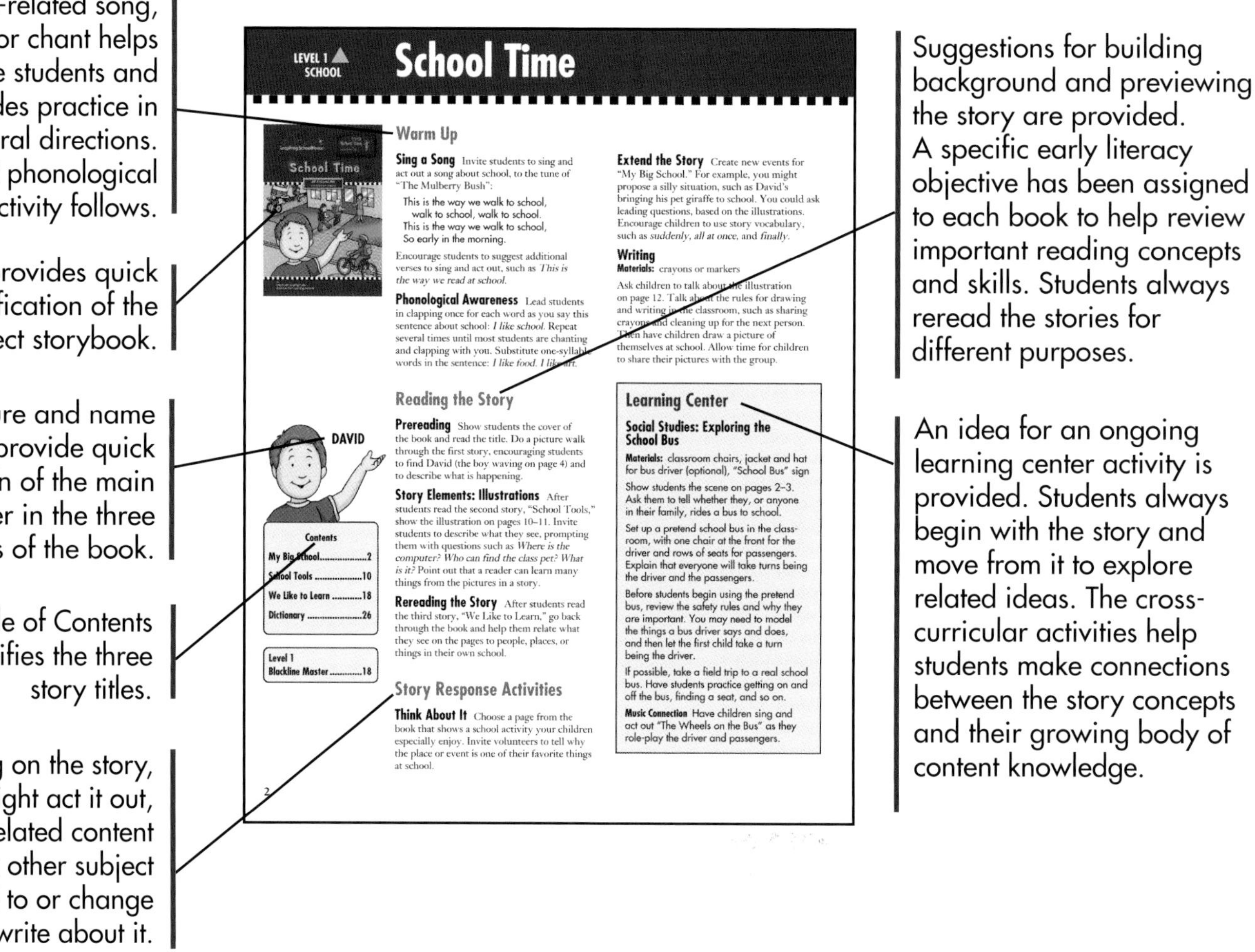

LEVEL 1 SCHOOL

School Time

Warm Up

Sing a Song Invite students to sing and act out a song about school, to the tune of "The Mulberry Bush":

This is the way we walk to school,
walk to school, walk to school.
This is the way we walk to school,
So early in the morning.

Encourage students to suggest additional verses to sing and act out, such as *This is the way we read at school.*

Phonological Awareness Lead students in clapping once for each word as you say this sentence about school: *I like school.* Repeat several times until most students are chanting and clapping with you. Substitute one-syllable words in the sentence: *I like food. I like art.*

Extend the Story Create new events for "My Big School." For example, you might propose a silly situation, such as David's bringing his pet giraffe to school. You could ask leading questions, based on the illustrations. Encourage children to use story vocabulary, such as *suddenly, all at once,* and *finally.*

Writing
Materials: crayons or markers

Ask children to talk about the illustration on page 12. Talk about the rules for drawing and writing in the classroom, such as sharing crayons and cleaning up for the next person. Then have children draw a picture of themselves at school. Allow time for children to share their pictures with the group.

Reading the Story

Prereading Show students the cover of the book and read the title. Do a picture walk through the first story, encouraging students to find David (the boy waving on page 4) and to describe what is happening.

Story Elements: Illustrations After students read the second story, "School Tools," show the illustration on pages 10–11. Invite students to describe what they see, prompting them with questions such as *Where is the computer? Who can find the class pet? What is it?* Point out that a reader can learn many things from the pictures in a story.

Rereading the Story After students read the third story, "We Like to Learn," go back through the book and help them relate what they see on the pages to people, places, or things in their own school.

Contents

Story Response Activities

Think About It Choose a page from the book that shows a school activity your children especially enjoy. Invite volunteers to tell why the place or event is one of their favorite things at school.

Learning Center

Social Studies: Exploring the School Bus

Materials: classroom chairs, jacket and hat for bus driver (optional), "School Bus" sign

Show students the scene on pages 2–3. Ask them to tell whether they, or anyone in their family, rides a bus to school.

Set up a pretend school bus in the classroom, with one chair at the front for the driver and rows of seats for passengers. Explain that everyone will take turns being the driver and the passengers.

Before students begin using the pretend bus, review the safety rules and why they are important. You may need to model the things a bus driver says and does, and then let the first child take a turn being the driver.

If possible, take a field trip to a real school bus. Have students practice getting on and off the bus, finding a seat, and so on.

Music Connection Have children sing and act out "The Wheels on the Bus" as they role-play the driver and passengers.

2

Using the Series

When first introducing the *All Around Me Storybook Series* to a group of students, be sure to show them how the LeapPad platform works. Demonstrate how to place the book on the LeapPad platform, turn on the power, and use the tip of the LeapPad pen to touch the GO circle on each spread and to touch the words and pictures.

Introducing a Book

Before students read a new book for the first time, tie its content into the theme you are exploring. One way to do this is to teach students the song, chant, or finger play that begins every lesson in the *Teacher's Manual.* Students will enjoy reciting and performing these short selections with each other and with family members at home.

Introduce and preview the actual book using the ideas in the Warm Up and Prereading sections of the lesson in the *Teacher's Manual.* After the preview, students can listen to the stories at their own pace.

Enjoying the Stories

You may want to have students read the stories independently using headphones. Another approach is to set up a center where two to four children read a book together, with one student navigating the page and the other students listening. Students might also use the book to have a tutoring session with an adult or older "reading buddy."

If the storybook reading is part of an ongoing theme, you may want to assign a specific story that ties in particularly well with a thematic concept students are currently exploring in other content areas.

Follow-Up

After students read and discuss the book, use the suggestions in the lesson section titled Story Response Activities. You may wish to display a copy of the book in a learning center where students can refer to it as they progress through the Learning Center activity provided in the lesson.

An important part of Follow-Up is the home connection. After students work with their blackline master activities, they can take them home to share what they have learned with their families.

School Time

Contents

Warm Up

Sing a Song Invite students to sing and act out a song about school, to the tune of "The Mulberry Bush":

This is the way we walk to school,
  walk to school, walk to school.
This is the way we walk to school,
So early in the morning.

Encourage students to suggest additional verses to sing and act out, such as *This is the way we read at school.*

Phonological Awareness Lead students in clapping once for each word as you say this sentence about school: *I like school.* Repeat several times until most students are chanting and clapping with you. Substitute one-syllable words in the sentence: *I like food. I like art.*

Reading the Story

Prereading Show students the cover of the book and read the title. Do a picture walk through the first story, encouraging students to find David (the boy waving on page 4) and to describe what is happening.

Story Elements: Illustrations After students read the second story, "School Tools," show the illustration on pages 10–11. Invite students to describe what they see, prompting them with questions such as *Where is the computer? Who can find the class pet? What is it?* Point out that a reader can learn many things from the pictures in a story.

Rereading the Story After students read the third story, "We Like to Learn," go back through the book and help them relate what they see on the pages to people, places, or things in their own school.

Story Response Activities

Think About It Choose a page from the book that shows a school activity your children especially enjoy. Invite volunteers to tell why the place or event is one of their favorite things at school.

Extend the Story Create new events for "My Big School." For example, you might propose a silly situation, such as David's bringing his pet giraffe to school. You could ask leading questions, based on the illustrations. Encourage children to use story vocabulary, such as *suddenly, all at once,* and *finally.*

Writing

Materials: crayons or markers

Ask children to talk about the illustration on page 12. Talk about the rules for drawing and writing in the classroom, such as sharing crayons and cleaning up for the next person. Then have children draw a picture of themselves at school. Allow time for children to share their pictures with the group.

Learning Center

Social Studies: Exploring the School Bus

Materials: classroom chairs, jacket and hat for bus driver (optional), "School Bus" sign

Show students the scene on pages 2–3. Ask them to tell whether they, or anyone in their family, rides a bus to school.

Set up a pretend school bus in the classroom, with one chair at the front for the driver and rows of seats for passengers. Explain that everyone will take turns being the driver and the passengers.

Before students begin using the pretend bus, review the safety rules and why they are important. You may need to model the things a bus driver says and does, and then let the first child take a turn being the driver.

If possible, take a field trip to a real school bus. Have students practice getting on and off the bus, finding a seat, and so on.

Music Connection Have children sing and act out "The Wheels on the Bus" as they role-play the driver and passengers.

Let's Go to School!

Warm Up

Recite a Chant Ask students to watch and listen as you perform this chant:

What can you see?
What can you see?
What can you see at school?
(Shade your eyes and look around.)

Pause to let several students tell what they see. Then continue by substituting actions and words for the other senses: *What can you hear/touch/taste/smell at school?*

Phonological Awareness Have students sit or stand in a large circle. Ask them to join in as you begin clapping slowly and rhythmically. When everyone is on the beat, clap once loudly and freeze. Then say a child's name, clapping once for each syllable. Repeat the name several times before saying and clapping another child's name.

Finding Parts of Speech Use the book to present a simple lesson on naming words and action words. Invite students to pantomime verbs such as *singing, talking, cleaning.* Have them point to nouns such as *chair, marker,* and *button.* Point out that some words name things and other words name actions.

Writing
Materials: chart paper and markers

Like Ana and her classmates, students have many important things to do at school. Invite the class to create several "To Do" lists, perhaps for art, science, and housekeeping. Record the lists on the chart paper. Then have students illustrate their lists on the chart paper.

Reading the Story

Contents

Prereading Show students the cover of the book and read the title. Talk about what the students and teacher are doing in the illustration. Ask volunteers to predict what the story might be about.

Story Elements: Characters After students have read one of the stories, talk about the main character, Ana. Page through the stories and ask different students to point to her in each scene. Tell students that the main character is the person a story is mostly about.

Rereading the Story Lead students in a pantomime of some of the things Ana does at school, such as riding a bike or eating lunch.

Story Response Activities

Think About It Display page 7 and have students tell how Ana's story time is the same as or different from their own story time. Continue with other scenes of the book.

Learning Center

Art: Shape Collage

Materials: small cutouts of shapes in different colors, glue, sheets of construction paper cut in triangle or circle shapes

Show and discuss the shapes on pages 14 and 26. Then model for students how to make a shape collage. Show them how you choose shapes and colors to include in your picture. Demonstrate how to put a single dot of glue in the middle of a small shape to make it stick to the collage.

As students work, encourage them to talk about the shapes and colors they are choosing. Remind them to write their name on the collage, or dictate the letters for you to write.

Set aside a time to share the pictures. Talk about how each artist arranged the shapes and colors on his or her collage.

Language Arts Connection Encourage pairs of students to take turns naming shapes and colors as they look at *Let's Go to School!* independently.

Look at Me!

Warm Up

Sing a Song Invite students to sing and act out "If You're Happy and You Know It."

> If you're happy and you know it,
> clap your hands *(repeat twice)*,
> If you're happy and you know it and
> you really want to show it,
> If you're happy and you know it,
> clap your hands.

Make up verses about other feelings, such as *sleepy/close your eyes* or *sad/cry boo-hoo.*

Phonological Awareness Lead students in clapping once for each beat in a child's name: E-liz-a-beth or Lar-ry. After students have clapped the beats in several names, have them count the claps in a short name such as Sam or Jamie.

Adding to the Story Invite students to imagine what Alex's bedroom might be like—is it big or small? Is it neat or messy? Help them use describing words to tell how things look, feel, and sound in his room. They can use words such as *happy, excited,* or *sleepy* to tell how Alex feels about specific things there.

Writing
Materials: crayons or markers, pictures of fruits and vegetables, small blank books

Like Alex in the story "What Alex Likes," students have likes and dislikes. Make a display of foods and invite students to tell which ones they like or dislike, and why. Then explain that each student will make a book about his or her favorite foods.

Contents

Reading the Story

Prereading Show students the cover of the book and read the title. Do a picture walk through the first story, encouraging students to describe how Alex looks and to name some things he likes to do.

Story Elements: Characters' Feelings
After students have listened to the second story, "Alex's Feelings," show the six pictures of Alex on pages 10–11. Invite students to name how the boy feels in each picture and to tell why they think so. Then have students act out different feelings as you point to the pictures.

Rereading the Book After students have listened to the third story, "What Alex Likes," go back through the book and have students relate special things about Alex to things about themselves.

Story Response Activities

Parts of Speech: Describing Words
Use "Who Is Alex?" to present a simple lesson on describing words. As you page through the story, invite students to use adjectives that tell what color or how many. Point out that color words and number words help you know how things look.

Learning Center

Math: Picture Graph

Materials: small slips of paper, pencils, tape, chart paper, pictures of 2 or 3 pets

Show students the scene on pages 2–3 of *Look at Me!* Ask them to tell about a family pet or a pet they would like to have.

Explain that you want to find out about students' favorite pets. Show them the animals they can choose from, such as a dog, a cat, and a fish. Each child can draw a favorite pet on a small slip of paper and write his or her initials.

While students are working, tape the three large pet pictures at the bottom of a sheet of chart paper. As students finish their pictures, help them find the large picture of their favorite pet and tape their small picture in a column above it.

Then ask students questions about their favorite kind of pet.

Health Connection Have students make other graphs based on the book *Look at Me!,* such as favorite foods.

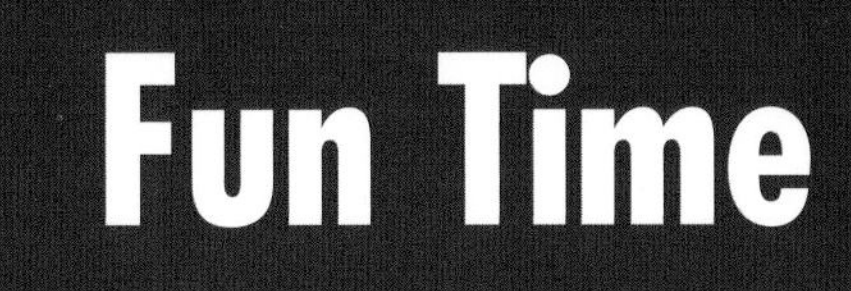

Fun Time

Warm Up

Act Out a Rhyme Ask students to watch and listen as you perform this chant:

I can bend, bend, bend,
I can hop, hop, hop.
I can twist, twist, twist,
I can stop, stop, stop.
(Coordinate actions with the words.)

Invite students to say and perform the words several times with you. Substitute other actions in the first and third lines, such as reaching, kicking, or bouncing.

Phonological Awareness Review with students that words like *hop* and *stop* are rhyming words—words that end with the same sound. Explain that you will say three words, and they are to listen carefully for the two words that rhyme. Begin with *hop, stop,* and *ball.* When most students name *hop* and *stop* as rhyming words, continue with other sets of words, such as *man/can/bug* or *cat/gas/hat.*

Contents

Reading the Story

Prereading Show students the cover of the book and read the title. Talk about what the girl is doing in the illustration. Ask volunteers to predict who the story might be about.

Story Elements: Title Page Have students look at the first page of the book. Explain that this page is called the title page. It shows the title of the story, the name of the author, and sometimes a picture from the story. Tell students that the girl on the title page is named Kelly and that she is the same girl shown on the cover.

Rereading the Book After students have read the stories, have them choose one to reread with a partner. Partners can take turns telling what Kelly and the other characters are doing on each page of the story.

Story Response Activities

Act Out a Story Ask students who play soccer to help you lead the class in acting out the story "Kelly Plays Soccer." Have students form a large circle around the soccer players. As you call out an action from the story, such as *kick* or *run*, the students in the middle can model each action (in place) for others to copy.

Sequencing Events Use the second story, "A Day at the Beach," to talk about *first, next,* and *last.* Turn to pages 10–11 and have students talk about what the family does first in the story. (They pack the car.) Continue through the rest of the story to talk about what happens next and last.

Think About It Display page 22 and have students tell how Kelly's bedtime is the same as or different from their own bedtime. Continue with other scenes in the book.

Learning Center

Science: Our Senses

Materials: objects that can be seen, heard, smelled, or touched (musical instruments, spice bottles, fabric swatches, etc.), four boxes, recording journal, colored pencils

Show the picture of Kelly on page 7 and use the labels to talk about how we see, hear, touch, smell, and taste.

Explain that you will put many objects in the science center for students to sort according to their senses. For example, they might put all the things that make sounds in one box.

After students have sorted the objects, have them record their ideas in a journal. Some students might draw the objects in groups, while others make word lists.

Language Arts Connection Encourage students to bring an item from home that appeals to more than one sense. Invite them to give a short oral talk about their object.

This Is My House

Warm Up

Learn a Finger Play Invite students to watch and listen as you perform this finger play to the tune of "Frère Jacques."

See my house, see my house,
(Form a square by interlocking fingers and bending hands at knuckles.)
Here's the roof, here's the roof.
(Make a triangle with two index fingers.)
Come inside with me,
(Open the "door" by spreading thumbs.)
Come inside with me, see my family,
see my family.
(Turn hands over and wiggle fingers to represent people.)

Phonological Awareness Say this sentence: *I have a family.* Ask students to clap once for each word they hear in the sentence as you say it again. Then count the claps together. Repeat with other short sentences.

Reading the Story

Prereading Show students the cover of the book and read the title. Give several students a chance to tell how their home is the same as or different than the home on the cover. Then do a picture walk through the first story, encouraging students to relate what they see to their own homes.

Story Elements: Setting After students have read the first story, show the cutaway of the house on pages 2–3. Explain that this house is the setting of the story, the place where the story happens. Help them match each story illustration to a room shown on pages 2–3.

Rereading the Book After students have read all the stories, invite them to name the items shown on page 26. Then they can find each item in one or more of the stories. The stove, for example, is on pages 5 and 17.

Story Response Activities

Think About It Have students take turns asking and answering questions, using the large scenes on pages 2–3, 10–11, or 18–19. For example, on pages 18–19, a student might ask, *What do you think is inside these wrapped boxes for Luis?* Students can use the illustration on page 24 to find the answers.

Parts of Speech: Nouns Tell students that naming words, or nouns, can name people, places, or things. Ask volunteers to find pictures of people in the book, such as the sister or father. Repeat with nouns that name places and things.

Writing

Materials: crayons or markers, paper scraps, scissors, glue

Have students compare Luis's birthday party with parties they've attended. Then ask them to imagine they are going to the party, too. They can use the art materials to make a gift for Luis. Encourage students to write or dictate a sentence telling about their gift and what Luis will like about it.

Contents

Learning Center

Social Studies: Model Home

Materials: large sheet of tagboard or building blocks, furniture catalogs or dollhouse furniture, scissors

Ask volunteers to help you build a simple one-story house with blocks. If you prefer, draw several rooms in a house on tagboard. Have students tell about the rooms in their house.

Explain that students will add furniture to the house, putting each piece in the correct room. If students are using dollhouse furniture, they can take turns placing one item in each room and telling why they put it there. If students are cutting pictures of furniture from catalogs, have them work with partners to find appropriate pictures and cut them out.

When the house is furnished, ask questions about how they chose to decorate or arrange the house.

Math Connection Have students make size comparisons between the rooms, using words and phrases such as *bigger than, smaller than, taller than,* and so on.

The Family Home

Warm Up

Sing a Song Make up actions to suit the words as you teach students "Five in the Bed," a subtraction finger play/song:

There were five in the bed
And the little one said, "Roll over! Roll over!"
So they all rolled over and one fell out.
There were four in the bed . . . etc.
(Coordinate actions with the words. The last line of the verse is "There was one in the bed, and the little one said, 'Goodnight!'")

Phonological Awareness Use a puppet for this activity. Explain that when you whisper a word in the puppet's ear, it will say the word very, very slowly.

Pretend to whisper a word such as *bed* in the puppet's ear. Have the puppet stretch the sounds in the word as it says /b/-/e/-/d/. Ask students to say the word as they would normally: *bed.* Repeat with other CVC words such as *dog, Pat,* and *sun.*

Reading the Story

Prereading Show students the cover of the book and read the title. Talk about what the family is doing in the illustration. Ask volunteers to predict who the story might be about and where it might take place.

Story Elements: Vocabulary After students read the first story, "Pat's Great Day," have them make a list of things they do at home indoors on rainy days. Compare their list to things Pat's family did in the first part of the story. Use the actions shown in the illustrations to extend students' speaking and viewing vocabularies.

Rereading the Book After students have read the stories, have them choose one to reread with a partner. Partners can take turns telling what Pat and the other characters are doing on each page in the story.

Story Response Activities

Social Studies: Economics Have students reread the second story, "Grandpa Moves In." Invite students who have grandparents living at home or nearby to relate the story to their own experiences. Ask students why Grandpa might have moved into Pat's house. Use the illustrations in the story to discuss everyone's need for food, clothing, and shelter.

Changing the Story Have students reread the third story, "Pat's Birthday." Ask them whether or not they would like to get a desk like Pat did for her birthday. Have students brainstorm other items that Pat might have received and make a list of their ideas. Students can retell the story to include one of the items on the list.

Think About It Choose a page from the book that shows a popular home activity, such as sitting together in the living room (page 17). Invite volunteers to tell why they like the place or event.

Learning Center

Art: Family Pictures

Materials: easel paper, paints, paintbrushes, smocks, pencils (optional)

Show the pictures of Pat's family on pages 10–11 and 18–19. Talk about the settings for the two pictures and how the artist filled each scene with color and interesting details.

Explain that small groups of students will paint pictures of their families. Talk about whether they will show their families outside or inside. You may want to have students sketch their picture with a pencil before using the paints. As students work, remind them to use the whole paper, to include every family member (even pets), and to add interesting details.

When everyone has had a chance to paint, let each student have a turn to show and tell about his or her painting.

Music Connection As students sketch and paint, play quiet music to set a peaceful, cozy mood.

Contents

A Trip Around Town

Warm Up

Sing a Song Invite students to sing this song about a neighborhood, sung to the tune of "Down by the Station":

Down at the library,
Early in the morning.
See all the people
With magazines and books.

Encourage students to name other places in a neighborhood to sing about, such as the post office, the bakery, or the park.

Phonological Awareness Say a short tongue twister such as "Silly Sidewalk Sally," and repeat it several times so that students can join in. If any students' names begin with /s/, use their names in the phrase. Ask a volunteer to suggest another tongue twister in which all the words begin with the same sound, such as *big blue bus*.

Reading the Story

Prereading Show students the title pages for the first story on pages 2–3. Talk about the places and people shown in the neighborhood. Then ask students to predict what the story will be about.

Story Elements: Words After students have read the first story, go back to page 4. Have students point to the words at the bottom of the page. Show students how to point to each word as it is said aloud, and ask them to do the same. Continue with other pages.

Rereading the Book After students have read all the stories, point out the repeated pattern in the first story: *This is my ___.* Have them take turns rereading the story with partners, using the language pattern and picture clues to read the words.

Story Response Activities

Health: Staying Safe Outdoors Have students look at one of the street scenes in the book to review safety rules for pedestrians. Use one of the park scenes to review how to use playground equipment safely.

Parts of Speech: Verbs Use the second story, "Fun at the Park," to present a simple lesson on verbs. Tell students that action words, or verbs, tell what people or animals do. Have students name the actions the children and animals are doing in the park, and then act them out.

Writing
Materials: crayons or markers, blank books

Have students reread the third story, "A Special Saturday." Invite them to write a story about a time they have gone downtown or to the mall with their family. They can use the story pattern *(I like ___. I don't like ___.)* for their own book.

Contents

Learning Center

Math: Build a Play Space

Materials: building blocks, index cards, markers, other props (cars, people, etc.)

Invite students to build a model of a playground that they would like to have in their town. First, brainstorm ideas for play areas, such as a jungle gym or bike paths and bridges. Some students might want to sketch their ideas first.

Let students experiment with different sizes and shapes of blocks to see what works best. Encourage them to make signs for their playground that show how to use the equipment safely.

Language Arts Connection Have students explain why they chose particular shapes and sizes of blocks for each part of their playground.

Neighborhood Fun

Warm Up

Action Chant Ask students to join in as you alternately clap your hands and slap your thighs. When everyone is on the beat, say this chant as you continue the actions:

> Where shall we go in the neighborhood,
> the neighborhood, the neighborhood?
> Where shall we go in the neighborhood,
> Who can tell us now?

Pause to let a volunteer name a place in the neighborhood and tell what he or she might do there. Then begin the motions again and repeat the chant for others to have a turn.

Phonological Awareness Review with students that words like *store*, *more*, *floor*, and *door* are rhyming words—words that end with the same sound. Say a sentence that contains two rhyming words, such as *A little mouse ran into my house*. Have students repeat just the rhyming words. Continue with other sentences. (Nonsense rhymes are acceptable in this activity.)

Story Response Activities

Social Studies: Geography
Materials: globe or world map

Have students reread the first story, "All Around Town." Tell students that Tian's aunt is from China. Show them China on the globe. Ask students how they think Aunt Lijun came to America to visit Tian.

Adding to the Story Have students reread the story "A Spring Festival." Ask them about neighborhood festivals or block parties they have been to, and what they did there. Students can add more events to the story, based on their knowledge of neighborhood festivals. Encourage them to use time-order words from the story, such as *first* and *then*.

Think About It Have students tell whether they would like to get a pet for their birthday like Tian did in the third story. Help them relate events in the story to special days they have spent with their families.

Contents

Reading the Story

Prereading Show students the cover of the book and read the title. Then show the title pages for the second story on pages 10–11. Talk about what is happening in the illustration. Then take a picture walk through the second story.

Story Elements: Plot After students read the third story, "Birthday Treasure Hunt," talk about how the story ends. Point out that Tian has to solve a problem in the story. She has to follow clues to find her new puppy at the end. Tell students that how a character solves a problem is called the plot of a story.

Rereading the Book After students have read the stories, have them choose one to reread with a partner. Partners can take turns telling what Tian and the other characters are doing on each page in the story.

Learning Center

Writing: Festival Posters

Materials: crayons or markers, posters and ads about community events

Show the festival scene on pages 13–16. Invite students to tell some of the things that people are doing at the festival, and which ones they would like to do.

Have students imagine that they are having a neighborhood festival. Tell them they are in charge of advertising the festival so that people will know about it. Display posters and ads from events in your community, and have students note how the words and the pictures make the event seem fun and exciting.

Students can work in small groups to make their posters. Before they begin, tell them to use about half their paper for pictures, and half for words.

Music Connection As students plan and write their posters, play lively music to create a festival mood.

Helping Hands

Warm Up

Learn a Finger Play Ask students to watch and listen as you perform this finger play. Repeat it several times, encouraging students to join in.

Hands on your knees
And hands on your toes,
Hands do the hard work,
Everyone knows.

Hands can wash
And hands can dry,
Hands can sweep
And hands can tie.
(Coordinate actions with words.)

Make up verses about other helpful things that we do with our hands. Repeat the first four lines after each verse.

Phonological Awareness Invite students to clap once for each beat in a child's name: Tan-ya, A-lex-an-der. You can also have them clap the beats in a classmate's first and last name: Sha-na Jack-son.

YOKO

Contents

Reading the Story

Prereading Show students the cover of the book and read the title. Do a picture walk through the first story, focusing on how Yoko is helping her dad. Have students relate this to their own experiences.

Story Elements: Illustrations Tell students that the pictures in a story can help a reader understand what is happening. As you page through the first story, "Taking Care of Dad," ask students how they think Dad feels. Have them tell how the illustrations help them know.

Rereading the Book Give students a purpose for rereading the second story. Ask them to find all the ways that Lily is helpful to others.

Story Response Activities

Sequencing Events Use the second story, "Lily Is a Good Helper," to talk about the time order in a story. Have students review what Yoko and Lily do before school. Pairs of students can take the roles of the two girls and act out the order of events in the story.

Social Studies: Community Helpers
Use the third story, "How Firefighters Help," to discuss the services firefighters and other helpers provide to people in a neighborhood. After reading the story, students can share what they know about firefighters.

Writing
Materials: old greeting cards, crayons or markers, construction paper

Ask students why Yoko made her dad a card in the first story. Display greeting cards and talk about why people send cards to each other. Tell students they can make a card for a friend or a family member. Show them how to fold a sheet of construction paper in half to make a card.

Learning Center

Health/Science: Making Orange Juice

Materials: oranges cut in half, manual juicer, strainer, small cups

Remind students that Yoko and her mom brought healthy foods like juice and soup to Yoko's dad when he was sick. Show students the materials and talk about how to make orange juice.

Let students take turns squeezing the juice from orange halves. You may wish to make a recipe chart that shows the steps in making juice. Post it in the center for students to read. Encourage students to help each other make the juice.

Math Connection Talk about *half* and *whole* as students squeeze the oranges. Serve orange quarters as snacks. Talk about *part* and *whole.*

Everyone Can Help

Warm Up

Act Out a Song Ask students to think about times they have helped someone else. Call on someone to tell how he or she has been a good helper. When the student is done, lead the class in singing this version of "For He's a Jolly Good Fellow":

For he's/she's a jolly good helper,
For he's/she's a jolly good helper,
For he's/she's a jolly good helper,
Now help me choose a friend.

On the last line, the speaker can choose a new student to have a turn.

Phonological Awareness Display a puppet and tell students that it likes to say words very, very slowly. Whisper a word such as *fun* in the puppet's ear. Have the puppet stretch the sounds in the word as it says /f/-/u/-/n/. Ask students to blend the sounds to say the word at a regular pace: *fun*. Repeat with other CVC words such as *cat, ten, hop,* and *sip*.

CARLOS

Reading the Story

Prereading Show students the cover of the book and read the title. Talk about what the people are doing in the illustration. Ask volunteers to predict who the stories might be about. Then ask volunteers to predict what might happen in the stories.

Story Elements: Author's Purpose Ask a volunteer to tell what an author does. Talk about favorite authors such as Margaret Wise Brown or Eric Carle. Tell students that an author always has a reason, or purpose, for writing a story. Read the title of the book and ask students what the author's purpose might be.

Rereading the Book After students have read the stories, have them choose one to reread with a partner. Partners can take turns telling how Carlos and the other characters are helping each other.

Contents

Story Response Activities

Think About It Have students make a list of ways they could help a new student feel welcome and comfortable in their classroom. They can compare their list to the ways Carlos helps Tim in the story "How Can I Help?"

Health: Bike Safety Use the second story, "Learning from Luis," to review bike safety rules. Students can make a chart that lists safe and unsafe behaviors. Invite volunteers to illustrate the chart.

Act Out a Story You will need stuffed animals as props for this activity. After students read "Helping Animals," let volunteers tell about their experiences at the vet's office. Use the illustrations in the story to review the ways that vets help animals. Then let students take turns role-playing Carlos and his dad, using the stuffed animals as the patients.

Learning Center

Writing: Books About Helping

Materials: blank books, crayons, pencils

In advance, write a short story about how you have helped someone in your role as a teacher. Read the story to students. After they have a chance to respond to your story, ask them to brainstorm ideas for other stories about helping. Stories can be about a single event or about things students do regularly to help their family, friends, teammates, or someone else. Encourage students to help each other think of ideas.

Have students write and illustrate or draw and dictate their stories.

Each day, ask a few authors to share their stories with the group. Then place the stories in the library center for everyone to enjoy.

Art Connection Encourage students to make covers for their storybooks. They can include a picture, a title, and their own names.

LEVEL 1
ANIMALS

Our Animal Friends

Warm Up

Learn a Finger Play Teach students this finger play:

Three little kittens were napping in the sun.
(Hold up three fingers of one hand; pretend to sleep.)
Four little puppies crept in for some fun.
(Hold up four fingers of other hand; pantomime creeping.)
"WOOF!" said the puppies, as loud as can be,
And the three little kittens ran right up a tree.
(Show three fingers running up other arm.)

Phonological Awareness Say pairs of words such as *pet* and *pal*. Ask students whether they hear the same sound at the beginning of both words. Repeat with other word pairs, including some that start with different sounds.

Science: What Animals Need Use the first story, "We Love Pets," to talk about what all animals need, including food, water, and air. Ask students who have pets to tell how they help their pets stay healthy and safe.

Act Out a Story Tell students they will act out some of the animals in the book, so they need to find a space in the room where they can move freely. If space is limited, you can let small groups of students take turns. Remind students that most animals make a distinctive sound (moo, bark, purr) and also move in special ways (gallop, swim, fly).

Reading the Story

Prereading Show students the cover of the book and read the title. Do a picture walk through the first story, inviting students to tell about pets they know.

Story Elements: Setting After students have read the last story, ask where Pa and Gram live. Explain that their farm is the setting of the story, the place where the story happens. Help them locate places on the farm on pages 24–25.

Rereading the Book Ask students to work in pairs to reread the second story to find an animal they want to learn more about. Students can research the animal and give a report about it to the class.

Story Response Activities

Changing the Story After students read the last story, ask them to imagine that Pa and Gram live in a forest or a desert instead of on a farm. Invite students to tell about new animals Liz might see and what might happen.

Learning Center

Science: Classifying

Materials: models or photographs of animals, science journals, pencils

Collect animal pictures or models that can be sorted in a variety of ways, such as by number of legs, color, body covering, habitat, or size. Have small groups of students decide how they will sort the animals. They can work together to make groups. When everyone is satisfied with how the animals have been sorted, ask students to record their ideas in a journal, using words, pictures, or both. Different groups can present their ideas to the class.

Math Connection Have students count the number of animals in each category they make.

LIZ

Contents

Animals Everywhere

Warm Up

Sing a Song Teach students this version of "A Hunting We Will Go":

A hunting we will go,
A hunting we will go,
We'll catch a mouse
And put her in a house,
And then we'll let her go.

Other animals to use in the song are fox (box), bear (chair), fish (dish), cat (hat).

Phonological Awareness Write the name *Bingo* on chart paper. Teach students the song about the farmer's dog, pointing to each letter as you sing it. Then model for students how to substitute a clap for the letter *B*. Continue by leaving out a letter and adding a clap each time you repeat the song.

Reading the Story

Prereading Show students the cover of the book and read the title. Talk about the animals in the illustration. Ask volunteers to predict what the stories in the book might be about.

Story Elements: Real and Make Believe Display *Animals Everywhere* alongside a make-believe animal story such as "The Three Pigs." Have students give reasons why the first story could happen in real life, but the other story could not.

Rereading the Book Have partners turn to the dictionary on pages 26–27. They can take turns naming an animal and then finding its picture in one of the stories they read.

Story Response Activities

Science: Animal Habitats Use the first story, "Beach Creatures," to talk about habitats. Students can make a chart of animals whose home is the beach or the ocean. Invite students to tell about other habitats, such as a forest, a desert, or a park.

Think About It Have students reread the second story, "At the Zoo." Ask them to note the differences among the groups of animals that the children visit. Students can vote for their favorite—reptiles, mammals, amphibians, or birds.

Sequencing Events Use the second or third story in the book to review story sequence. Students can find time-order words like *first, next,* and *last* in "At the Zoo." They can tell what happens in the beginning, middle, and ending of "A Very Special Field Trip."

Learning Center

Writing: Beach Big Book

Materials: large sheets of paper, crayons or chalk, pencils

Write this sentence frame on the chalkboard: *I see ___ at the beach.* Ask students to suggest several animals' names to write in the blank. They can refer to the first story, "Beach Creatures," for ideas.

Explain that everyone will contribute a page to a class big book about the beach. Each child can draw a beach or ocean creature on their paper, leaving space at the bottom to copy the sentence from the board. Tell students to put the name of their creature in place of the blank. They can help each other or use a dictionary or the story to spell their creature's name.

Assemble the pictures in a big book and ask a volunteer to illustrate the cover. After sharing the book, put it in the library center for everyone to enjoy.

Science Connection Encourage students to find out more about their animals by looking through nonfiction picture books or visiting the school media center.

Contents

Nature's Wonders

Warm Up

Sing a Song Teach students this version of the song "It's Raining, It's Pouring":

It's raining, it's raining,
When I wake up, it's raining.
I jump out of bed and bump my head
and look outside, it's raining.

Substitute other weather words in the song, such as *sunny, windy, snowing.*

Phonological Awareness Say a compound word such as *treehouse* or *snowman.* Ask students to repeat it with you, clapping for each part of the word. Then ask, *Did you say* mehouse? *Did you say* bowman? Have students correct you. Repeat the question with other sounds at the beginning of a word. Once students have the idea, let them take turns changing sounds.

Reading the Story

Prereading Show students the cover of the book, and read the title. Do a picture walk through the first story, inviting students to tell what they like to do outdoors.

Story Elements: Vocabulary Use the third story, "Sara Plants a Seed," to show students how illustrations can help them with unfamiliar vocabulary words. Have them connect the last word in each sentence to something in the picture.

Rereading the Book Point out the repeated pattern in the second story: *I see a* ___. Have students take turns rereading the story with a partner, using the language pattern and picture clues to read the words.

Story Response Activities

Act Out a Story Lead students in acting out "Winter at the Park." Begin by pantomiming putting on winter clothes. Continue with actions such as walking to the park, sledding down a hill, and so on.

Writing Write the names of the seasons on chart paper, and have students tell what they like or dislike about each one. Show pictures from the book of different things Sara did in summer, fall, winter, and spring. Students can draw and/or write about something they do in a particular season.

Science: How Plants Grow Use the last story, "Sara Plants a Seed," to talk about what plants need in order to grow. Discuss the stages a plant goes through. Ask students to tell about their experiences growing things.

Contents

Learning Center

Science: Observing

Materials: variety of fruits and vegetables, hand lenses, scale for weighing, science journal, pencils

Take a short field trip to observe plants growing at school. Help students describe the plants they see, using color and size words. Encourage them to compare plant parts, such as leaves and bark, on different plants. Encourage children to use the hand lenses to observe things closely "in the field."

Back in the classroom, students can observe similarities and differences among fruits and vegetables. Have them use hand lenses to examine them closely. They can use the scale to make further observations. They can choose one item to draw and label in a journal.

Math Connection Have students weigh each food and then put the food in order from heaviest to lightest.

LEVEL 2 ▲▲
NATURE

A Nature Walk

Warm Up

Learn an Action Chant Make up actions and sound effects to suit the words in this version of "Going on a Bear Hunt." Tell students to repeat each line, sound, and action after you:

Let's walk in the forest.
Listen to the wind in the trees.
Listen to the chattering squirrels.
Oh no! A stream! We'll have to swim!
Oh no! Tall grass! We'll have to go through it.

Keep going to other places in the forest, perhaps including a bear's cave.

Phonological Awareness Say pairs of words such as *rock* and *rain*. Ask students whether they hear the same sound at the beginning of both words. Repeat with other word pairs, including some that start with different sounds.

TRAVIS

Contents

Reading the Story

Prereading Show students the cover of the book, and read the title. Talk about the forest and the animals shown. Ask volunteers to predict what the stories in the book might be about.

Story Elements: Dialogue Display page 9. Ask students to name the two characters who are talking to each other. Read the text and have students note that some of it is the exact words that the two characters are saying.

Rereading the Book Ask students to work in pairs to reread the first or second story to find an animal they want to learn more about. Students can research the animal and give a report about it to the class.

Story Response Activities

Think About It Invite students to tell about a forest they have walked through or seen in a movie. Have them tell what they saw, heard, felt, and smelled in the forest. Students can relate their experiences to the stories in the book.

Cause and Effect Display page 17 and read the text. Ask students why the children are running and why their hair is blowing. Explain that dark clouds and wind *are causing* everyone to run inside before it rains. Turn to page 20 to have students see what happens next.

Extending the Story Have students work in small groups to enact what happens next after rereading "A Rainy Day." They can be as imaginative as they like, acting the parts of rainbows, floods, a snowstorm, as well as the characters' responses to these events.

Learning Center

Math: Measure and Compare

Materials: large tub or water table, variety of measuring cups and spoons, containers of various sizes and shapes, water

Review the rules for working at the water table. Tell students they can use different containers to pour, measure, and hold water.

After students have had time to experiment on their own, have them solve problems that you write on index cards. For example, have them find out how many tablespoons of water will fill a quarter-cup measuring cup. Then have them find out how many teaspoons of water will fill up the same container. Help them explain their findings.

Science Connection Students can observe evaporation by placing a shallow container of water in the sun for a few days.

Food Fun

Warm Up

Learn a Chant Ask a volunteer to help you model the two-person clapping sequence for "Pease Porridge." After students have practiced in pairs, add the following words:

Pease porridge hot,
Pease porridge cold,
Pease porridge in the pot
Nine days old.

Phonological Awareness Teach students the first verse of the song "Apples and Bananas," in which the fruit names are said normally. Then choose a new vowel sound, such as long *e*, to replace short *a* so that the words *apples* and *bananas* become /eeplz/ and /beeneeneez/.

Parts of Speech: Verbs Use the second story, "Shani the Chef," to present a simple lesson on action words. Invite students to pantomime the action words as they reread the story. Review that action words like *measure* and *pour* tell what people are doing.

Act Out a Story Have students tell about times they have tasted foods that are salty, spicy, or sour. As they reread the third story, "Picnic in the Park," have them pretend they are tasting what Shani is tasting and act out her reactions.

Reading the Story

Prereading Show students the cover of the book, and read the title. Give several students a chance to tell which foods they like or dislike. Then ask them to predict what the book will be about.

Story Elements: Characters Ask students to name the main character in the book. Point out Shani's name on page 5, and have students find it on other pages in the book. Review that the main character is the person the story is mostly about.

Rereading the Book After students have read all the stories, invite them to name the items shown on pages 26–27. Then they can find each item in one or more of the stories.

Story Response Activities

Think About It Have students choose partners. They can take turns asking and answering questions about one of the stories, using the large scenes on pages 2–3, 10–11, or 18–19.

Learning Center

Health/Science: Trying New Foods

Materials: variety of foods that are sweet, salty, spicy, and sour, chart paper, markers

Ask parent volunteers to bring in simple foods for a tasting party. Encourage students to try at least one food from each taste category. (Please be sensitive to any special dietary requirements.)

When everyone has had a chance to try the foods, talk about how each food tasted. Divide the chart paper into four sections, and write a describing word in each section: *sweet, salty, spicy, sour.* Students can write the food names or draw pictures to categorize the foods by taste.

When the chart is finished, ask questions such as *How many foods were salty? Which foods were sweet? Which food was your favorite? Why?*

Art Connection Display paintings and photographs of foods in the center.

Contents

LEVEL 2 ▲▲
FOOD

Let's Eat!

Warm Up

Sing a Song Teach students these words to the tune of "Hush Little Baby":

I like pancakes,
Yes, I do!
I like pancakes,
What about you?

After students answer the question, invite them to suggest another food to sing about.

Phonological Awareness Say a compound word such as *pancake* or *eggshell*, and have students repeat it after you. Then change the final sound: say *pancape* or *eggshelf*, for example. Ask students how you changed the word. Other words to use are *gumball* and *meatloaf*.

Social Studies: Cultures Use the second story, "Food Fiesta," to talk about foods and traditions in different cultures. Invite students to tell about special foods they share with their families. Help them identify how their experiences are similar to or different from Juan's.

Writing Let students taste two or three foods at snack time, such as grapes, carrot sticks, and pretzels. Encourage them to tell what they like or dislike about each food, and then decide which one is their favorite. Students can make a picture graph showing their favorites among the three foods. (Be sensitive to any dietary restrictions.)

Contents

Reading the Story

Prereading Show students the cover of the book, and read the title. Have students tell what is happening as you take a picture walk through the first story.

Story Elements: Vocabulary After students read the second story, "Food Fiesta," have them make a list of things their family does in the kitchen. Compare their list to things Juan's family did. Use the story to extend students' speaking and listening vocabularies.

Rereading the Book After students have read the stories, have them choose one to reread with a partner. Partners can take turns telling what Juan and the other characters are doing on each page in the story.

Story Response Activities

Extend the Story Have students reread the first story, "Family Feast." Point out that the family goes to visit Juan's grandparents. Ask students to brainstorm other activities Juan might do in the new town, and other meals he might cook or eat with his family.

Learning Center

Social Studies: Good Table Manners

Materials: child-sized table and four chairs, four place settings, plastic foods

Show the picture of Juan's family sitting at the table on page 9. Ask students to tell about good table manners and to explain why each rule is important. Write the rules as students talk about them.

Show students the props, and explain that small groups will have a chance to role-play having a meal together. Help them decide who will set the table, who will serve the food, and who will clean up afterward. You may want to have students take turns being family members.

When everyone has had a chance to participate, review the list of rules. Have students relate each rule to the role-playing activity.

Math Connection Have students count the utensils and dishes before they set the table.

Travel Time

Warm Up

Act Out a Finger Play Ask students to join in as soon as they can on the actions and the words in this finger play:

Here is the engine,
(Hold up one fist.)
Here is the track.
(Hold other arm out straight.)
The engine moves forward
And the engine moves back.
(Coordinate actions with words.)
Now the bell rings!
Now the horn blows!
Watch this train as it goes and goes.

Phonological Awareness Recite a nursery rhyme such as "To Market, to Market." Invite students to repeat each line after you. Then change the first sound in the words: *Boo barket, boo barket,/ Boo buy a bat big/* . . . etc.

Reading the Story

Prereading Show the cover of the book, and read the title. Do a picture walk through the first story, inviting students to tell about ways they travel.

Story Elements: Table of Contents Show the title page and point to the Contents box. Tell students that some books have a table of contents. It tells a reader where to find stories in a book.

Rereading the Book Have partners turn to the dictionary on pages 26–27. They can take turns naming a vehicle for the other student to find in the book.

Story Response Activities

Health: Staying Safe Use the first story, "Hector on the Go," to talk about safety equipment such as bike helmets and life vests. Have students tell how each piece of equipment keeps people safe when they're in a vehicle.

Changing the Story After students read the last story, ask them to imagine that Hector's family is traveling in a plane or a boat instead of a train. Invite students to tell a new story about their trip.

Act Out a Story Tell students they will act out ways to travel, so they need to find a space in the room where they can move freely. If space is limited, you can let small groups of students take turns. Call out the name of a vehicle and encourage students to show how it moves and sounds.

Learning Center

Science: Design a Vehicle

Materials: photographs of vehicles; scrap materials made of plastic, wood, cardboard, etc.; modeling dough; toy wheels or buttons; toothpicks

Display pictures of vehicles, including futuristic ones, if possible. Encourage students to observe similarities and differences among the vehicles. (Explain the term *vehicles*.)

Show the materials, and invite students to tell how they could be used to create a vehicle. Demonstrate the properties of a few items, and have students tell which ones would be good for different vehicle parts, such as wheels, seats, or wings.

Have students work in small groups to create vehicles. When the vehicles are finished, invite students to demonstrate how their models move and what they can do.

Music Connection Teach students action songs such as "The Wheels on the Bus" or "Take You Riding in My Car."

HECTOR

Contents

LEVEL 2 TRAVEL

Here, There, and Everywhere

NAN

Contents

Warm Up

Sing a Song Sing "Row, Row, Row Your Boat." Then ask students to suggest another way to travel, and sing the song again like this:

Drive, drive, drive your car/van/truck,
Quickly down the street.
Ha, ha, we're having fun,
A car/van/truck is really neat.

Phonological Awareness Have a puppet lead students in saying the word *go* a few times. Then ask the puppet to listen as you segment the sounds in the word: /g/ - /ō/. The puppet can pretend to be confused so that students repeat the segmented sounds for it to hear. Repeat with other words such as *van, bike,* and *boat.*

Reading the Story

Prereading Show students the cover of the book, and read the title. Then show each story title page. Ask volunteers to predict what the stories might be about.

Story Elements: Author and Illustrator Have students tell what an author does and what an illustrator does. Ask them why the words and the pictures are both important in a story.

Rereading the Book Give students a purpose for rereading. Have them read to decide which type of transportation is their favorite, and why.

Story Response Activities

Think About It Have students relate Nan's adventures to their own traveling experiences. Students can also tell which picture shows something they would like to try, such as riding a horse (page 6) or paddling in a tube (page 23).

Social Studies: Geography Use the illustration on page 8 to discuss words that indicate relative location. Prompt students with questions such as *Which vehicle is far away? Which vehicle is near? Who is riding in the front seat? What is behind the blue truck?*

Parts of Speech: Nouns Review with students that nouns are words that name people, places, and things. On chart paper, make a three-column chart labeled *People, Places, Things.* Students can write nouns from the story in the appropriate columns.

Learning Center

Writing: Travel Big Book

Materials: large sheets of paper, crayons, pencils

Write this sentence frame on the chalkboard: *I like to ride in a* ___.
Ask students to suggest several vehicles' names to write in the blank. They can refer to the book for ideas.

Explain that everyone will contribute a page to a class big book about going places. Each child can draw a vehicle and then fill in the appropriate background, such as a street, the ocean, or the sky. Tell them to leave space at the bottom to copy the sentence from the board. Students can write the name of their vehicle in place of the blank, using a dictionary or the story to spell the word.

Assemble the pictures in a big book and ask a volunteer to illustrate the cover. After sharing the book, put it in the library center for everyone to enjoy.

Social Studies Connection Students can research their vehicles on the Internet or in picture books.

Name ______________________ **Theme: School, Level 1**

Directions: Have students talk about the scenes and compare them with places in their own school. Then model how to give clues about one picture for children to guess. Partners can take turns asking each other riddles about the scenes.

Name ______________________________ Theme: School, Level 2

1. Color.

2. Cut.

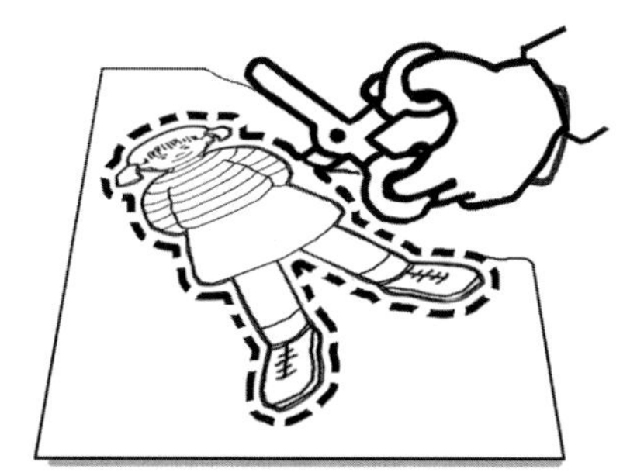

3. Glue.

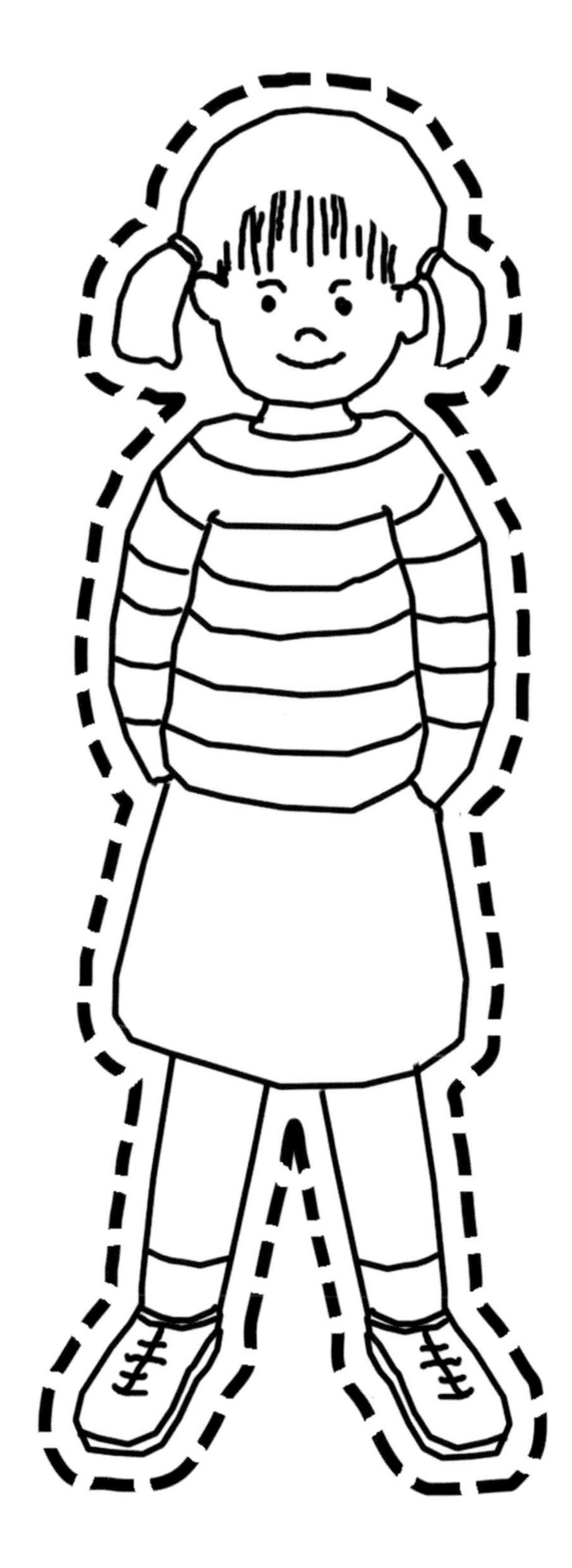

Directions: Tell students they will make a stick puppet of Ana, the main character in the story. Have them color the puppet before cutting it out. Help them glue the stick puppet on a craft stick, leaving some of the stick for a handle. When the glue is dry, students can use the puppet to tell stories about Ana's day at school.

Name ________________________________ Theme: About Me, Level 1

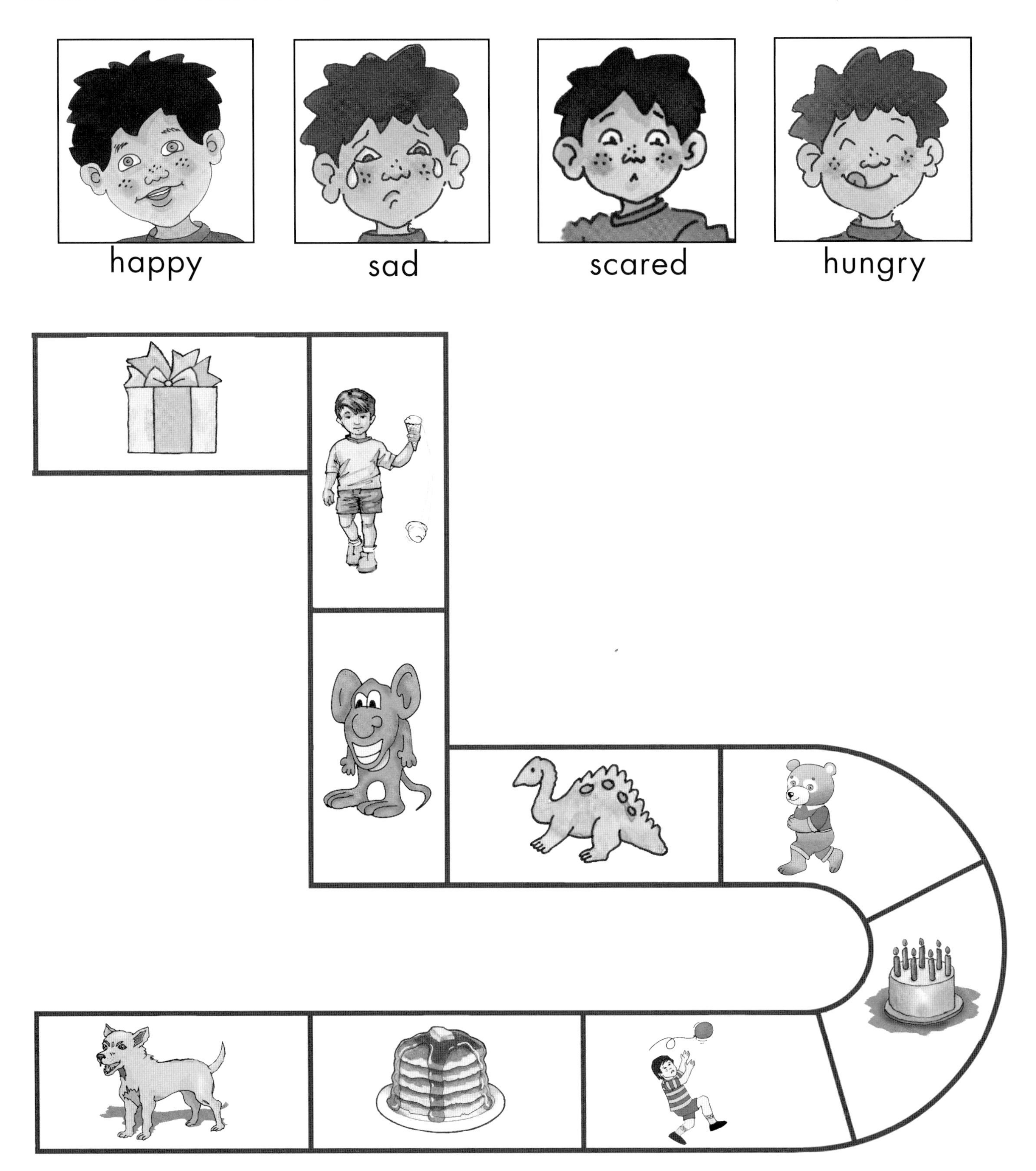

Directions: Ask students to pantomime how Alex feels as they point to each of the four faces. Then have students "walk" their finger (or a game piece) along the path, telling whether they like or dislike each picture, and how it makes them feel. Students can draw more pictures on the back for partners to tell about.

Name ______________________________

Directions: Students will need small cars or other markers for this activity. Have them reread "A Day at the Beach." Working with a partner, they can take turns "driving" from Kelly's house to the beach. Students can tell stories about what they see along the way.

Directions: Have students color Luis and his dog before they cut out the two figures. Model for students how to tell a story about Luis (or his dog) after placing him in one room of the house. Partners can tell each other riddles about different rooms and indoor activities.

Name ______________________________ **Theme: Home, Level 2**

Directions: Have students use the four panels to retell the story "Grandpa Moves In." Then have them cut out the panels, mix them up, and put them in the correct order to tell the story to a partner. Students may wish to color the pictures before they cut them out.

Directions: Have students color and cut out the figure of Mark. Model for students how you can tell a story about Mark as you move the cutout to the playground or along the street. Partners can ask each other riddles about places in the neighborhood.

Name ______________________________

Directions: Have students use the six panels to tell the story "A Spring Festival." Then have them cut out the panels, mix them up, and put them in the correct order to retell the story to a partner.

Directions: Have partners take turns choosing a person or animal to talk about. Students can identify the problem and tell what they could do to help.

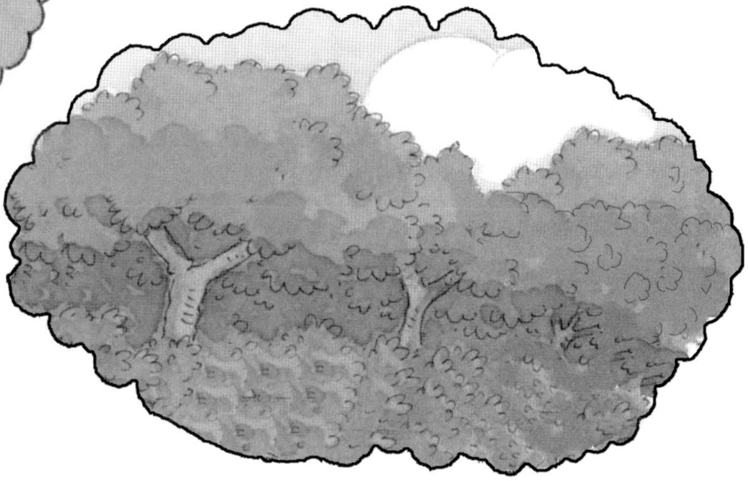

Directions: Have students color and cut out the figure of Carlos on his bike. They can move Carlos around in the scene, finding two safe places for him to ride his bike and two places when he shouldn't ride at all. Have students tell why each place is safe or unsafe for someone on a bicycle.

Name ______________________________ **Theme: Animals, Level 1**

Directions: Have students talk about the scenes or ask each other riddles about some of the details. In the scene at the pet store, students can draw a new pet for Liz.

Name ______________________________ **Theme: Animals, Level 2**

Directions: Have students cut out the animal cards and paste them in the beach scene. Then invite students to imagine they are walking on the beach. Have them tell what they see.

Name ______________________________ **Theme: Nature, Level 1**

Directions: Have students work in pairs. Give each pair a button or chip to toss onto the page. When the chip lands on or close to a picture, the student names the season and tells one fact about it.

Name ______________________________

Theme: Nature, Level 2

Directions: Students will need game pieces or markers for this activity. Have them imagine they are in the forest with Travis and his class. Working with a partner, they can take turns telling what they see as they "hike" from the bus to the ranger cabin.

Name ______________________ Theme: Food, Level 1

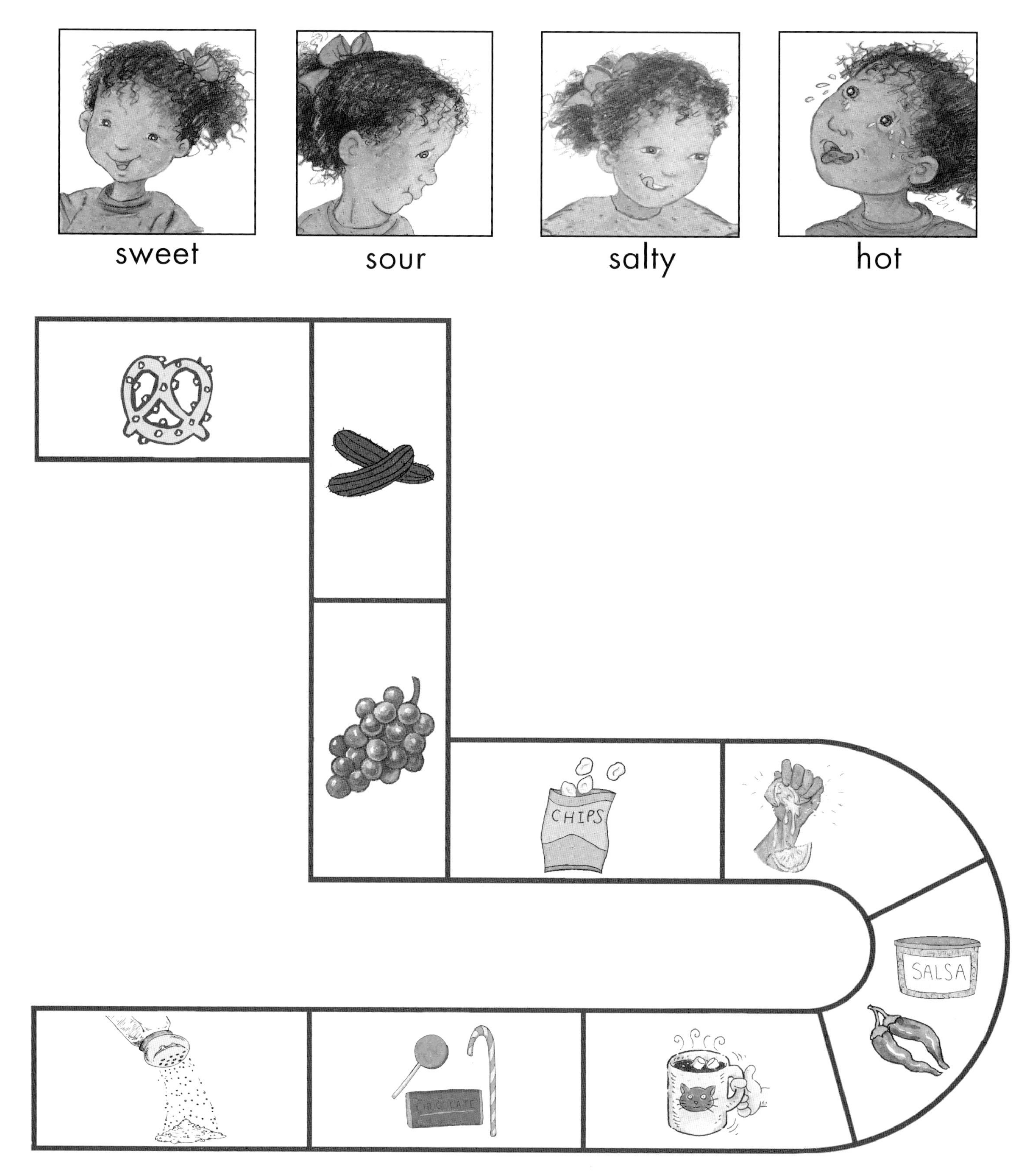

Directions: Review the tastes represented by the four faces. Then have students "walk" their fingers (or a game piece) along the path, telling how each food tastes and whether or not they like it. Students can draw more foods on the back for partners to tell about.

Directions: Have students use the six panels to tell the steps in making burritos. Then have them cut out the panels, mix them up, and put them in the correct order to retell the steps to a partner. On the backs of the panels, students can draw the steps in making a food they like.

Name ______________________________ **Theme: Travel, Level 1**

Directions: Have students color and cut out the vehicle cards. They can sort them in various ways, or combine cards with a partner to play Concentration or Go Fish. Some students may want to make additional vehicle cards.

Name ________________________ Theme: Travel, Level 2

Directions: Have students cut out the vehicles and paste each one where it belongs in the scene. Then invite them to imagine they are taking a trip. They can tell which vehicle they are riding in and describe what they see and hear.

The LeapTrack™ Connection

Enhance the learning opportunities of the *All Around Me Storybook Series* with the LeapTrack system, our assessment and instruction program.

The LeapTrack system allows teachers to quickly assess each student's skills, pinpoint areas for improvement, and create a personalized learning path across reading, language arts, and math.

Using the LeapTrack system with the *All Around Me Storybook Series* will allow teachers to do the following:

Assess students efficiently throughout the year

- Using the LeapPad® platform, students complete skills assessments in reading, math, and language arts.

Generate informative and actionable reports to monitor student progress

- The LeapTrack system scores student activity on assessment books and provides detailed reports to guide further instruction.
- Reports can be printed, emailed, or viewed in an electronic format.

Prescribe individualized, engaging instruction including the *All Around Me Storybook Series*

- Based on the results of their assessment, students are prescribed an appropriate, individualized learning path. Part of that learning path may include the *All Around Me Storybook Series*, based on the skills each individual student needs to further practice.

Ensure mastery of skills

- Performance on the prescribed instructional material, including the *All Around Me Storybook Series*, is scored by the LeapTrack system to ensure that the student has learned the skills covered in the content.

To find out more about using the LeapTrack system in your classroom, please call 1-800-883-7430.